The Story of

Homes

Monica Hughes

www.raintreepublishers.co.uk
Visit our website to find out more information about **Raintree** books.

To order:
☎ Phone 44 (0) 1865 888112
🖹 Send a fax to 44 (0) 1865 314091
🖥 Visit the Raintree Bookshop at **www.raintreepublishers.co.uk** to browse our catalogue and order online.

First published in Great Britain by Raintree, Halley Court, Jordan Hill, Oxford OX2 8EJ, part of Pearson Education. Raintree is a registered trademark of Pearson Education Ltd.

Editorial: Sian Smith
Design: Kimberley R. Miracle, Big Top and
  Joanna Hinton-Malivoire
Picture research: Ruth Blair
Production: Duncan Gilbert
Illustrated by Beehive Illustration
Originated by Dot Gradations

Printed and bound in China by Leo Paper Group

ISBN 978 14062 1006 4 (hardback)
ISBN 978 14062 1016 3 (paperback)

12 11 10
10 9 8 7 6 5 4 3 2

British Library Cataloguing in Publication Data
Hughes, Monica
  The Story of Homes
  1. Housing - History - Juvenile literature 2.
Housing -   Juvenile literature
  I. Title
643.1'09

Acknowledgments
The publishers would like to thank the following for permission to reproduce photographs: ©Alamy pp.19 (Alistair Balderstone), 9 (Gareth Byrne), 12 (Michael Jenner) 4 bottom (Paul Thompson Images) 14 (Robert Haines); ©The Art Archive p.18, 7 (Gianni Dagli Orti); ©Corbis pp.10, 16 (Bettmann), 17 (Douglas Hill, Beateworks), 8 (Elizabeth A. Whiting; Elizabeth Whiting & Associates) 13 (Richard Hutchings), 11 (81A Productions) ; ©Getty Images pp.15 (ImageBank) 6 (Stone); ©istockphoto.com pp.5,5; ©Pearson Education Ltd pp.5 (Debbie Rowe), 4 (Phillip Bratt); ©source unknown p.4

Cover photograph reproduced with permission of ©Corbis (Bettmann)

Every effort has been made to contact copyright holders of any material reproduced in this book. Any omissions will be rectified in subsequent printings if notice is given to the publisher.

Contents

Some words are printed in bold, **like this**. You can find out what they mean in the glossary.

Homes today

Semi-detached houses.

Terraced houses.

Detached houses.

Your home is the place where you live. There are lots of different types of homes. Some are houses that are **detached** and stand on their own. Some houses are **semi-detached,** where two houses are joined together. There are **terraced** houses, which are long rows of houses joined together.

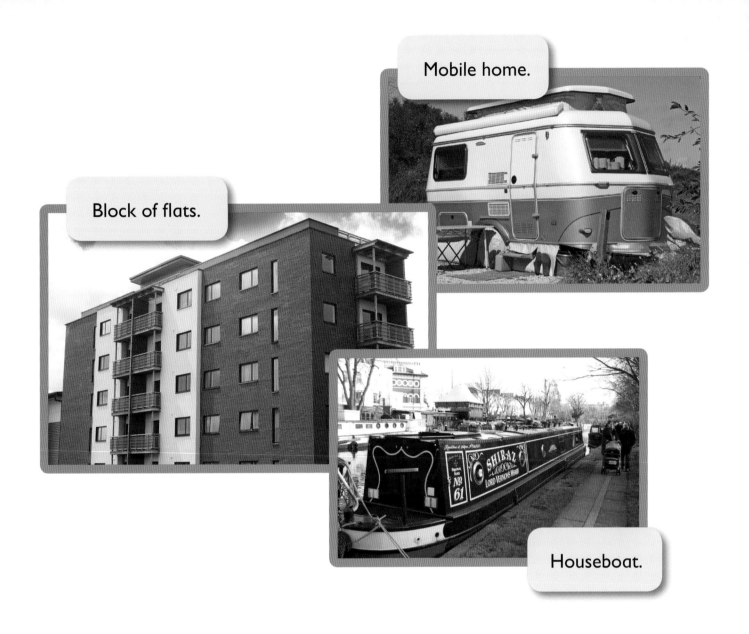

Mobile home.

Block of flats.

Houseboat.

There are **bungalows** and blocks of flats. There are caravans, mobile homes, and houseboats. Homes come in many shapes and sizes. Some houses are very small. Some houses are really big. These are all just buildings unless people live in them and then they become homes.

Old and new buildings

thatch

Some people live in houses that are new. They have only just been built. Some people live in houses that were built a long time ago.

The house in this picture was built a very long time ago. It has a **thatched** roof. This means that the roof is covered with straw.

tiles

These houses were built a long time ago, in a time called **Victorian** times. They are made from brick and the roofs are covered with tiles.

In this book we will look at what these Victorian houses were like long ago, when people first lived in them. We will see how they were different from homes today.

Hallways and rooms

A Victorian hallway.

The first room in a **Victorian** house was the hallway or hall. From the hall, people could get to the stairs and to other rooms inside the house. People in Victorian times thought that the hall was an important room.

This house has just been built. It has a few big rooms instead of lots of small rooms.

Things are different in many houses today. Instead of having a hall and lots of small rooms, some houses have a few big rooms and no hall. The stairs may go down into a large living room. There can also be a place for eating or cooking in the same room.

Living rooms then and now

A Victorian parlour.

Victorians had a room called a **parlour**, where they could sit with people who came to visit. Parlours had lots of pictures on the walls, books to read, and some had a piano.

In Victorian times, there was no **electricity**. Coal and wood were burned in a fireplace to make the room warmer. Candles and gas lamps were used for light.

A living room today.

In many homes today, the living rooms are warm and bright. There are electric lights and most houses have radiators to keep the rooms warm. In the living room, there might be a sofa or some chairs. There is often a television and a computer.

Kitchens then and now

A Victorian kitchen.

Kitchens have changed a lot over the years.
In **Victorian** times kitchens were dark because
there was no **electricity**. There was a large
cooker called a **range**. The range became hot by
burning coal. Victorians had to do many jobs by
hand, such as washing clothes and washing dishes.

A kitchen today.

In kitchens today, we have many machines
that help us to do different jobs. Most of these
machines use electricity to make them work.

We have kettles that heat up water, and
microwaves and toasters that heat up food.
We also have machines that wash dishes, and
machines that wash and dry clothes.

Bedrooms then and now

A Victorian bedroom.

Victorian bedrooms were cold and dark. There was a coal fire to heat up the room. They had a candle or an oil lamp to light the room. The bed was made from metal and had sheets and blankets. Under the bed was a **chamber pot**. Many bedrooms also had a jug and bowl for washing.

A bedroom today.

Today bedrooms are often warm and bright. Some people listen to music, watch television, and even use a computer in the bedroom. These days most people have duvets rather than blankets on the bed. Wardrobes and drawers are used to store clothes and toys in.

Bathrooms then and now

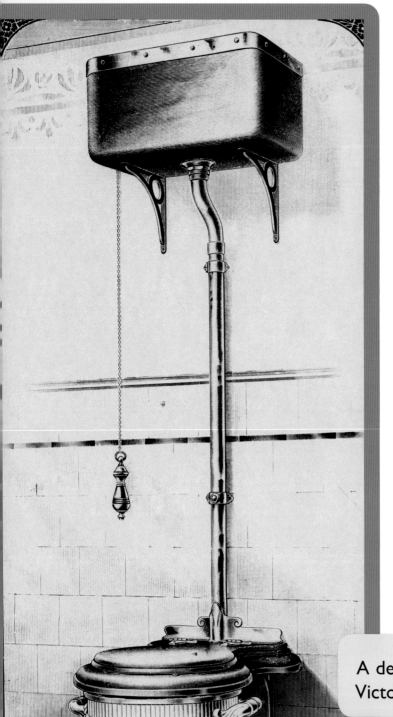

The bathroom is the room where people wash themselves and go to the toilet. Long ago, some rich **Victorian** people did have a bathroom. They would have had a bath in it and a **decorated** toilet.

Most homes would not have had a bathroom. They had a toilet outside the house called a **privy**. A bath made of tin was put in the kitchen. This was used for people to wash in.

A decorated Victorian toilet.

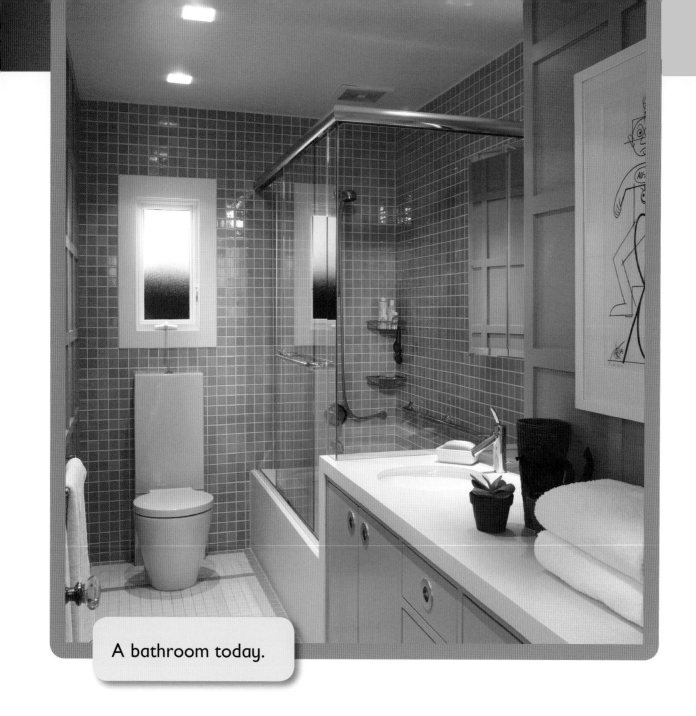

A bathroom today.

Most homes today have a bathroom inside the house. Many homes have more than one bathroom. In bathrooms today there is usually a toilet, a sink, a bath, and a shower.

Gardens then and now

terraced house

yard

A Victorian yard.

Long ago in **Victorian** times, large houses had big gardens. The gardens had grass where people could play games. They often had a place for growing vegetables.

Many homes at that time did not have a garden though. **Terraced** houses had a small back **yard** rather than a garden. The ground was covered with brick or stone.

A garden today.

Today there are gardens of all shapes and sizes.
Houses that are built today often have a small
garden. Do you have a garden? How is your
home different from homes in the past?

Teachers' guide

Because reading ability varies so widely in Year 1, we suggest this book is used in the following way. Read the book through as a whole class activity. Then do the following activities, using the book as a resource at each point, as indicated. The activities will benefit from using a variety of images of homes from various time periods, as well as the images in the book. This will allow you to cover the QCA guidelines as fully as possible with as many children as possible.

ACTIVITY 1

- Look at pictures of various types of home. Discuss various ways to describe them (try to find examples of as many of the following examples as possible): by size; by style: flat, terraced, semi-detached, detached, bungalow; by age: old, very old, modern; by particular terminology: caravan; tent. Use the images on pages 4 and 5.

- Choose 3 different images from your examples and discuss the features of the home: doors, windows chimneys, etc. Label these features and display the labelled pictures.

ACTIVITY 2

- Take a class walk through the streets near the school, looking at various homes. What can you tell about them from the outside? Split the class into groups, each with a chart to collect information about the houses. Do they vary, or are they all built to the same pattern? Are they big or small? Do they look old or new? What are they made from? What are the doors made from? What about the windows? Are the windows big or small? Are there windows in the roof? Are the homes terraced, semi-detached, detached, etc. Do they have front gardens? Have the children make a rough sketch of one of the homes, with notes on the features. Collate the charts back in the classroom and see if there are any exteriors in the book that match any of the homes you have been looking at. Draw up their own homes.

ACTIVITY 3

- Compare the homes on pages 6 and 7. Consider building materials, size of windows, chimneys (what does that tell you about heating). Move on to compare a modern home and an old home from the pictures you have collected: both exteriors. If possible, try to compare like with like, not a Victorian mansion with council flats now or Victorian workers cottages with a Sandbanks mansion. Brainstorm a list of their similarities and differences.

ACTIVITY 4

- Work through the book comparing the living rooms, kitchens, bedrooms and bathrooms. Discuss similarities and differences. Consider what the pictures don't show, too: how are the rooms heated/lit? Encourage the children to look at the detail: it is harder to spot the bed in the modern picture, but it's there.

ACTIVITY 5

- Use a large picture of a Victorian or Edwardian home. Divide the children into as many groups as there are rooms in the house. Each group has to tell a short story about the room, mentioning as many of the objects in it as they can. From this point, you are focussing on either Edwardian or Victorian homes. (The book focuses on a Victorian home.)

ACTIVITY 6

- QCA suggests that the children should have an opportunity to handle Victorian or Edwardian household objects (such as a flat iron). Local museums do sometimes loan out (or visit with) household objects such as these. Alternatively, a pre-arranged school trip might provide an opportunity to handle the items (this would need to be arranged beforehand). Various historic houses around the country also take school groups to dress up and handle artefacts, if pre-arranged.

ACTIVITY 7

- QCA suggest you transform the home corner into one room in an Edwardian or Victorian house. If this proves too difficult, you could make a modern room and then display a photo and description of the Victorian version and contents next to the modern one (iron, bed, etc).

Find out more

Books

Life in the Past: Victorian Homes, Mandy Ross
(Heinemann Library, 2004)

Start-Up History: Homes, Stuart Ross
(Evans Brothers Ltd, 2002)

Then and Now: Life at Home, Vicki Yates
(Heinemann Library, 2008)

What Was It Like in the Past? Homes, Mandy Ross
(Heinemann Library, 2003)

What is It Like Now? At Home, Tony Pickford
(Heinemann Library, 2002)

Websites

www.bbc.co.uk/education/dynamo/history/stepback.htm
Follow cartoon characters back in time to explore what a house
was like one hundred years ago.

www.museumofchildhood.org.uk
This museum in London has displays about toys and childhood.

Glossary

bungalow house that does not have an upstairs

chamber pot pot rather like a large potty used for going to the toilet in

decorate make something look nicer or more interesting by putting patterns on it

detached a detached house is one that is not joined on to another house

electricity energy used for lighting, heating and making machines work

parlour Victorian sitting room

privy toilet outside the house

range large cooking stove

semi-detached a semi-detached house is one that is joined on to another house on one side

terraced a terraced house is one that is joined on to other houses on both sides

thatched roof made of straw or reeds

Victorian from a long time ago when Queen Victoria was queen of Britain

yard piece of land attached to a house often covered with brick or stone

Index